A Party for Teddy

Barbara Mitchelhill

Series Editor: Louis Fid

Contents

Shopping

bread

butter

cheese

'I'm going to the shop.
This is my list,' said Mum.

'I'm going to the shop.
This is my list,' said Teddy.

bread and cakes

'I can get the bread,' said Mum.

'I can get the cakes,' said Teddy.

bread and cakes

Mum put the bread in the trolley.

Teddy put the cakes in the trolley.

'I can get the butter,' said Mum.

'I can get the sweets,' said Teddy.

Mum put the butter in the trolley.

Teddy put the sweets in the trolley.

'I can get the cheese,' said Mum.

'I can get the ice cream,' said Teddy.

Mum put the cheese in the trolley.

Teddy put the ice cream in the trolley.

Teddy and Mum went to the checkout.

'Look at all the shopping,' said Mum.

'We can have a big party,' said Teddy.

'Yes, we can,' said Mum.

Teddy likes shopping

Teddy can get the cakes. He is at the shop.
Stop, Teddy, stop. Stop, Teddy, stop.

Teddy can get the sweets. He is at the shop.
Stop, Teddy, stop. Stop, Teddy, stop.

Teddy can get the ice cream. He is at the shop.
Stop, Teddy, stop. Stop, Teddy, stop.

Party fun

'Come to my party. We can have fun,'
said Teddy.

'Come to my house,' said Teddy.

'This is my mum and dad.
This is my house,' said Teddy.

'Please have some cakes,' said Mum.

'Please have some ice cream,' said Teddy.

'Please come and dance,' said Teddy.

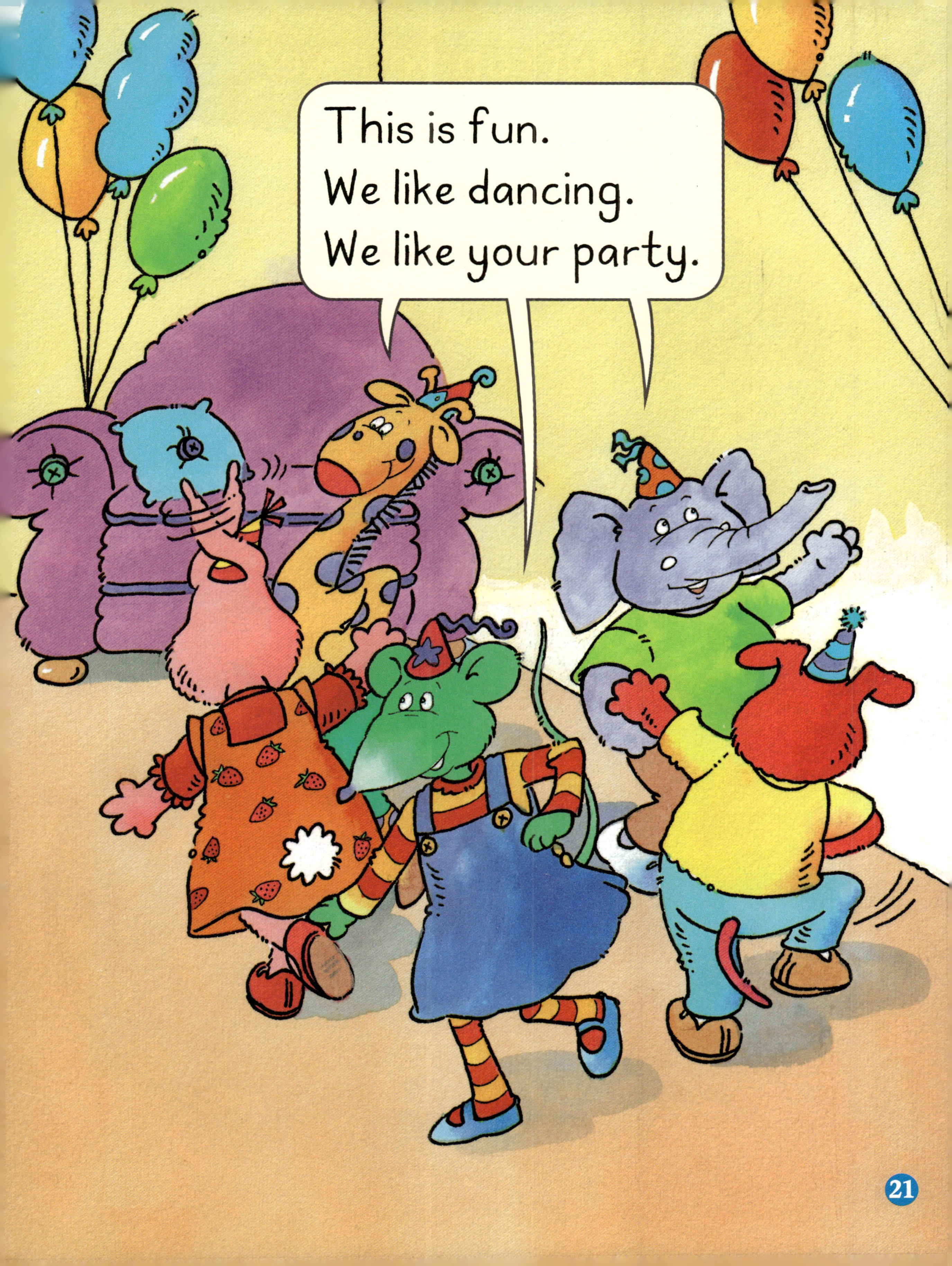
This is fun.
We like dancing.
We like your party.